MICE
AS A NEW PET

RICHARD PFARR

CONTENTS

W9-BAL-005

Photos by Dr. Herbert R. Axelrod, H. Bielfeld, Michael Gilroy, E. Jukes, H. V. Lacey, and Claudia Watkins.

4347589

Introduction

This book will introduce you to a new animal hobby: mouse-keeping. It will explain how to house, care for, breed, and train your mice. It will answer questions for which no satisfactory answers have been given and which are sure to arise as you progress in your hobby.

There are two types of mice raised today: the fancy mouse and the laboratory mouse. Countless thousands of laboratory mice have been bred for research work and laboratory experiments.

The fancy mouse came into prominence around the year 1900, when Walter Maxey, with the aid of a group of English fanciers, formed the National Mouse Club in that country. Prior to that time mice had been kept as pets, but no great attempt was made to standardize color and type. It is significant to add that at this time the works of Gregor Mendel were rediscovered. With the aid of his study of genetics, much of the guesswork in animal breeding was eliminated, and the course of breeding these little pets was made simple and easy to predict.

Since that time, the mouse fancy has been able to present over 60 different colors and varieties to pet lovers and fanciers. Size and type have been standardized and color and temperament improved to the extent that the fancy mouse has been able to claim its rightful

The mouse is a clever little creature that can make an interesting pet.

place in the hearts of fanciers. Its inquisitive, trusting nature and merry disposition enable it to compete for attention wherever it is shown.

All of this is written with the knowledge that as you take up the care and breeding of fancy mice, you will be providing yourself with an interesting and profitable hobby. Experience gained from breeding the various colors and varieties will enable you to enter into an intelligent discussion of genetics and color breeding. Indeed, you may be able to correct some of the common misconceptions held by quite a few animal breeders.

By nature, mice are keenly inquisitive and love to explore nooks and crannies.

Their small size and easy manageability have made mice the pet of choice for many people.

Feeding

The grain or pellets fed to mice are usually put on the floor of the run compartment. This is a satisfactory way to feed if the cage is cleaned at least once a week and the mice eat all the food given them in about ten minutes. Any leftover food will be stepped upon and become contaminated, so be sure that they consume all food and that none is left over. Mice become most active at dusk and stay awake until the early morning hours. An evening feeding time is suggested. If they are fed during the day, they will learn to follow such a schedule, but they will eat only enough to satisfy a small appetite and will waken again at night and be hungry. If you cannot feed them in the evening, you should leave a small surplus so that the mice will not be continually hungry during the night. To prevent this surplus from being contaminated, it should be placed in a small container.

Much of the satisfaction of belonging to an animal fanciers' group is derived

Proper nutrition is essential for all animals, and mice are no exception.

from following the traditional rules and methods handed down through the years. The time-tested diet of the fancy mouse has been a traditional one established by past generations of fanciers. As tradition has been a treasured part of the mouse fancy, strict adherence to the rules has always been a part of the game. For this reason, few attempts have been made by the majority of mouse fanciers to change the diet used and advocated for years.

Mice have continually growing teeth, which must be worn down by gnawing on hard substances. Good quality hard grains and leafy hay or grasses will supply the necessary material that mice must have. Without this, they will turn their attention to the exposed parts of their cages to keep their teeth trimmed. Mice are omnivorous, meaning that they will eat both vegetable and animal foods. This ability, characteristic of most other members of the rodent family, allows mice to survive under almost any condition. While they will

eat and enjoy a wide variety of foods such as cheese, meat scraps, and strawberry jam, the use of such foods is frowned upon, as they do not contain the proper amounts of minerals and protein. The consistent use of a plain wholesome diet is strongly recommended. It should consist of whole oats, good quality hay, and cubes of stale bread soaked in water. Several times a week, give your mice a treat of millet or canary or budgerigar seed. Some fanciers also feed fresh garden greens, while others never do, as this food causes digestive upsets if fed in too

A mouse that is well-fed will be active and attentive.

and efficient alternative to the traditional "homemade" diet. This is a pelleted food that contains every known ingredient necessary for the complete health of the mouse. This food was developed for use in laboratories that breed and raise thousands of mice annually. This food has been formulated for the exclusive use of mice and rats, and must not be confused with other pellet foods such as rabbit pellets or dog food.

These mouse pellets are suspended in small wire baskets that prevent the mice from contaminating them. Sometimes they are marketed in the form of cubes or small biscuits. Water is supplied by the familiar gravity-fed waterer with a curved glass or metal tube extending into the cage. The floor of the cage is kept dry in this manner, and using the waterer will reduce the incidence of disease to an absolute minimum. Cleanliness and ease of feeding are the main advantages in the use of this system. In addition, enough feed and water can be

Mice are fairly easy to feed because they enjoy a wide variety of food. Just remember that you shouldn't feed your pet too much of anything at one time.

large amounts or if it is introduced too quickly. Some mice enjoy eating greens while others ignore them completely.

Now, with this discussion of conventional foodstuffs in mind, let us consider another method of feeding mice which, while being a comparatively recently introduced diet, has already proved itself to be a modern supplied to keep the mice content in their cages for several days.

Use common sense in determining the amount of food that is served. In general, most mice do not gorge, so let your pet have a reasonable serving of food each day. A nursing female (doe) should be fed all she can eat, as the youngsters create an enormous demand upon her system. In hot weather, your mice may be unusually thirsty.

The use of waterers will prevent needless torment to the caged creatures, and you will be content knowing that you have given your charges the best chance for survival.

Fawn satin mouse. A well-balanced diet will be reflected in your mouse's overall appearance.

Housing

The building or area housing your mice is called a mousery. It can be large or small, depending upon the available space and the money you have on hand to invest in it.

For the sake of convenience, an enclosed area 6 feet by 6 feet would be the minimum size recommended for your mousery. This could be a building by itself or a fenced area within a garage or outbuilding. A separate room having a large window facing to the south would be ideal. However, the ventilation that the window affords is of

much more importance than the sunlight it gives the room. Mice are nocturnal animals, meaning that they are creatures of the night. A mouse exposed to direct sunlight is extremely uncomfortable and nervous and will desperately try to find a way to hide, as instinct

tells it that it can be seen and preyed upon.

Drafts and dampness will kill more mice than disease ever will. In fact, disease thrives in dampness, so if you eliminate dampness you will automatically help prevent germs from getting a foothold in your mousery. Proper ventilation, without cross currents or drafts, will dispel any dampness generated by quick temperature changes. Seal any cracks or small holes to prevent the escape of runaways.

Several shelves fixed to the wall will be needed as a holding area for the breeding boxes. A large box with a hinged lid can be used to store feed, hay, and shavings

Your mouse's housing should be located in a spot that is well ventilated and draft-free.

Replace your pet's bedding on a regular basis.

and can also be used as a bench when the lid is closed.

All the breeding boxes should be the same size to present a neat and uniform appearance. The measurements of the ideal breeding box should be 10 inches high, 10 inches wide, and 16 to 18 inches long. Mice are accomplished acrobats and can jump 6 inches with little effort, so the 10-inch height will prevent them from jumping out when the lid is opened.

A typical box is made of white pine shelving lumber, which can be bought in a standard 10-inch width, making the boxes easy to cut out and assemble. The top and one end have a 4-inch-square hole covered with one-quarter inch mesh screen wire stapled to the inside surface to prevent the mice from gnawing the exposed edges. A partition the size of the box ends, inserted 6 inches from the back end, will partition off the nesting quarters from the run compartment. Cut a 2-inch hole in one end of the partition 2 inches from the floor level, allowing easy entrance for the adults but acting as a barrier to the youngsters in the nest. The lid should fit inside the box; two cleats nailed to the top outside edges will keep the lid in position without sliding.

Put a layer of pine shavings in the run compartment of the box. This will give a warm underfooting and absorb any moisture. Soft hay should be placed in the nesting compartment on top of the layer of shavings. Between cleanings the nesting compartment should not be disturbed unless it is necessary to handle one of the occupants.

A trio of mice in a compartment will generate a surprising amount of warmth, as they will curl together in a ball, and their combined warmth will protect them from a reasonable degree of cold. During excessively cold weather, the nesting area should be filled to the top with hay for protection. Of course, with a nursing doe the nesting material should not be changed, as this intrusion on her privacy may cause her to desert her litter.

However, if you have handled your mice previously, they will soon learn to trust you and you can make a change if the shavings become damp.

Many generations of mice will pass their entire lives caged in this manner, all the while being content and healthy. They will come to know your footsteps and will invariably come out to meet you, as they are entirely dependent upon you to care for their every need.

The most practical way to house mice is in all-metal unit cages. The sliding bottom trays can be removed quickly and cleaned with ease. Such units can be purchased at pet shops.

Blue Fox mouse. The more time you spend with your pet, the more it will come to accept your presence.

Breeding

The fancy mouse is among the least expensive of mammals that you can buy, so there is no reason why you should not choose the very best when selecting foundation stock. What is required of a good fancy mouse might be described in

this manner: it should have a long, narrow, racy body suggesting graceful movement, and it should be tight-muscled with somewhat delicate bone structure, tulip-shaped ears, prominent eyes, and a long, well-proportioned tail.

A stud mouse will father the litters of at least six does, two of which will be in the breeding pen, two in the maternity pens, and two will be junior does kept until of breeding age. In a properly supervised breeding program, these does will produce sixty young in a year, so the quality of the buck must be of the very best to ensure a reasonable amount of quality youngsters. On an average, less than 20 percent of these will be suitable for future breeding stock, although an exceptional buck will throw a much larger percentage of fine mice.

It is difficult to judge the worth of a junior buck, for his type and color will continue to develop until after the first adult molt. Keep only the very best of your young stock and allow them to grow to adulthood before you make a final selection. In the case of the marked varieties, this choice can be made at a very early age, as the quality of the markings is the chief point to aim for. Let us assume that you have three young bucks to choose from, the rest having been gradually eliminated as their faults appear before this time. Put them on a table to judge them. Let us imagine that these mice are self blacks, as the selfs are the most difficult to judge. A common failing in all mice is in the length of the tail: it should be as long as the body. Use a ruler to measure the tail, as a quarter of an inch can be a deciding factor. Does it have a good "set-on" and does it taper to a fine whip-lash end? In ears, you must look for large size coupled with an up and forward appearance—tulip-shaped. Eliminate wrinkled or creased ears and those that tend to lay flat. The eyes should create an illusion of alertness, and be bold and prominent. Width of skull between the ears is a sure sign of later large size.

Does your choice have the desirable "Roman nose" muzzle with the nose looking

as if it were stuck on with a bit of glue? The body should be long and shaped like a stretched out question mark . . . a trifle arched over the loins. Does it have strong, but not coarse, bone structure? Sleek, smooth-lying fur, with the color going down to the skin, should influence your final choice.

Grading female mice is more difficult than judging male mice, for it seems that most does possess better type than bucks, making the choice a narrow one. A doe

A mouse breeding box. Ventilation has been provided for both on the lid and on the actual box.

13

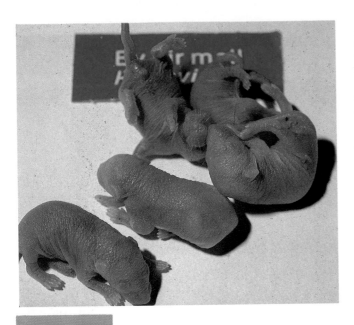

At birth, baby mice are blind, naked, and deaf.

Eliminate those that have unsound coloring or a few tan hairs on the flanks, around the vent, or behind the ears. The whiskers should be long, straight, and well spaced. Other than these suggestions, follow those outlined in the selection of stud mice.

A trio of mice consisting of a buck and two does is usually kept in a breeding box. The useful breeding life of a mouse seldom exceeds 18 months, so be sure your newly purchased trio is about 12 weeks old. If a record is kept of the day the trio is put together, the arrival of the litters can be easily predicted. On the 17th day the obviously pregnant does should be placed in maternity pens. This will allow them to settle down in their new quarters and get their homes in order for the new arrivals.

Soft grasses closely resemble the materials used in the wild state. The doe will work to assemble the nesting material into a hollow ball, making an entrance hole near the top of the nest. The litters are

will retain her style and type long after the male has grown stocky with coarse fur. Those fanciers of another day must have had the doe mouse in mind when they compiled the standard of excellence. The buck is readily distinguished from the doe because of his heavier build and his external sex organs. Never breed from does that have a masculine appearance or from bucks that are too delicate or feminine looking. A doe needs plenty of space in the body cavity to properly carry her young, so don't select those with extremely narrow hips.

commonly born during the daylight hours, most often in the late afternoon. That night the doe will stay in the nest, not making her regular appearance at feeding time. Don't disturb her at this time but see that she has a good supply of food and water.

On the second night entice her from the nest with a tidbit of food. Her slim figure will remove any doubt that the litter has arrived. Carefully open the top of the nest and remove any dead or undersized young. There will be an average of six per litter, but as many as 16 have been observed in a nest. While it is advised that each litter should be culled to a maximum of four, wait until

A mother mouse and her young. Mice are capable of mating as early as five to six weeks after birth.

the fifth day, when the doe will have developed a full supply of milk. At this time hair will begin to form on the naked young mice and the pigment contrast of the marked varieties can readily be seen and the mismarked young can be culled. Self-colored mice present a different problem, as they have no distinctive coloring at this time, but such obvious faults as white toenails and tails can be seen. The young mice open their eyes at nine days and venture out of the nest within two weeks. The doe will continue to nurse the litter for five weeks, and they will be weaned when six weeks old.

Now the young bucks must be taken from the maternity cage and put in separate cages. Some young bucks can remain with each other for a few more weeks, but all male mice will eventually fight with each other and many bitter battles will be fought. Battling males will frequently be sterile, as they attempt to foul each other. The young does will seldom fight, and those kept for future breeding can run with the mother for another two weeks, after which the doe can again be put in the breeding pen. Large numbers of does can be kept in a single cage, as they get along well with each other, but the disadvantage to this is that they cannot be

A successful breeding program should begin with the selection of good quality stock.

16

identified then and no accurate records can be kept. Therefore, keep the sister does together as a unit until they are adults and ready for the breeding pens. Two litters can run together if they are of different colors that serve to tell them apart.

Sometimes a doe will kill

instinct, so guard against sudden noises in your mousery. However, extreme thirst seems to be the chief reason for this fault, and the use of water bottles will just about exclude this from happening in your mousery.

When a trio is first put together the does may

Mice are amazingly adaptable animals that can flourish in a variety of environments.

her entire litter. This can be very disheartening if the litter was of an expected high quality. Several reasons have been advanced for the doe killing, or cannibalizing, her litter. Fright sometimes causes the mother to display an overly protective maternal

quarrel, but they will soon settle down and become a happy family within a few hours. Should one doe persist in quarreling with another doe, the buck will separate them and even punish the offending doe in order to make her adopt a more compatible nature.

At the start, you must decide upon a type of breeding program that will best suit your needs, and records must be kept to further the understanding of the results of that program. To make it workable, you must keep the colors separate to avoid indiscriminate breeding. The three types of breeding are: inbreeding, linebreeding, and crossbreeding. As crossbreeding introduces unknown qualities in the unrelated parent stock, it should be resorted to only when your mice show a consistent lack of a certain point of quality.

Inbreeding utilizes the closest of family relationships, such as father to daughter and brother to sister. Line-breeding is a modified version of

An Albino mouse with her babies. Newborns should be disturbed as little as possible.

inbreeding; related parents are used, but they are not as closely related as those used in the art of inbreeding. Of the three types, inbreeding will produce the fastest and most dramatic results, and it is the quickest way to complete success or failure. A cardinal rule that must be complied with is that no two parents possess the same fault. With closely related stock to work with, the fancier has mice with the same good and bad points. The theory is that if the breeder is observant, he can eliminate those mice showing undesirable traits and retain only the good qualities as they make their appearance. The theory of inbreeding does work in practice, and this fact will refute the claims of those who insist that inbred stock will gradually lessen in vigor and quality. Physical weakness, as well as poor color and type, can be eliminated. As each mouse must be compared with another before selecting them as parents, inbreeding is sometimes aptly called comparative breeding.

Fostering Young

If a mouse that has given birth is unable or unwilling to care for her young, you can provide the youngsters with a foster mother. In this way, they will be able to receive the care and nurturing necessary for their development.

Female mice have a highly developed maternal instinct and under proper conditions do an excellent job of rearing their litters. The does constantly clean the young and stay in the nest with them except when eating.

The tiny babies with sharp teeth fasten themselves to a teat, and should the doe leave the nest when one is nursing, it will travel with the mother. When this happens the youngster is immediately returned to the nest.

For an experiment, place a newborn mouse in the sight of another nursing doe. As soon as she sees it she will pick it up by the back of the neck and carry it off to her nest. There she will examine and thoroughly wash it and care for it as if it were her own, regardless of how many

are already in the nest. If two does litter together, they will make no distinction as to which litter they will nurse. As one doe may even attempt to nurse the combined litters, make sure that each doe carries her share of nursing the young.

Contrary to popular belief, the strain of nursing a litter until it is weaned is much harder on the constitution of the mother than conceiving and producing that litter. Consequently, some fanciers remove the doe as soon as the young are born and place them with a foster mother. This is usually a doe that has proved herself capable of rearing a litter, although she will not be of good enough quality to be used as a breeder. Such females are called wasters or cull does.

These foster does should be mated at the same time you mate your breeding stock, preferably a day sooner. When the more valuable litter arrives, remove the cull youngsters and replace them with the litter of wanted mice. Rub your fingers in a pinch of the shavings from the cage of the foster doe and she will be none the wiser for the exchange. Keep several of these foster does on hand; if there are no foster mice for them to rear, let them raise their own litter to maturity.

Another advantage to such "extras" is that they can be used to keep valuable stud bucks in condition, as males go out of condition in a short time if they are caged alone. A single mouse will be miserable in cold weather, as mice rely upon numbers to keep the nest warm in the cold months.

When adults pass the prime of their life, they become less active and exceedingly tame. Many a mousery has a few of these faithful older mice, and they are allowed free run in the mousery during feeding time. They will not venture far, and this daily outing gives them a new zest for life.

This page: Mice are perky, energetic little animals that will amuse you with their antics.

Opposite: If you are going to let your pet roam freely about the house, you should always be nearby to supervise him.

Color Breeding

The many colors evident in the fancy mice of today originated from one color—that of the wild mouse, commonly called Agouti. This coat color is common to other wild animals such as squirrels and rabbits. It is actually a combination or pattern of colors, and a close observation will reveal a band of black pigment at the base of the hairs, followed by a center band of chocolate, with the tips of the hairs showing yellow. This pattern indicates that the Agouti mouse has in it all the known colors of the recognized varieties. This wide variation of colors in fancy mice came into being through the effects of mutations that can be simply described as distinct changes from the original.

Color mutations can also be defined as a lessening of a dominant color or the complete absence of color as seen in the Albino or Pink-eyed White mouse. All color mutations, when viewed in their true position on a scale, will be found to be a lessening of the intensity of an original color. Starting with the Self Black, it could end with the extreme dilution of the Cream mouse. If a color chart could be pictured in your mind, you would be able to place each color in its relative position much as you would compare paint color samples in a paint color chart. The bold coloring of the Chocolate mouse is reversed to give us

Better stock is just as easy and inexpensive to keep as the less expensive animals.

When selecting mice for breeding, it is essential to choose animals that are sound and healthy.

the pastel shade of the beautiful Champagne mouse. In addition, some colors can be produced with either pink or black eyes, spotted or two-toned coats, and in some cases, three-toned. For the experimental breeder the choice is practically unlimited.

Undoubtedly you have heard of dominant and recessive colors. As a safe rule, the darkest colors are dominant and the lighter colors recessive. Every mouse has a color inherited from both parents. Purebred mice inherit the same color from both parents, but mice with a mixed ancestry will exhibit the dominant color

from one parent and possess the hidden recessive color of the opposite parent. Using purebred parent mice, a Black to Chocolate mating will produce young mice of solid black color, although 75% of them will then carry the chocolate color as a recessive hidden in their make-up. This tells us that a dominant color trait need be inherited from but one parent, while a recessive color must be inherited from both parents.

To illustrate this point, offspring in a black litter carrying recessive chocolate, when mated together, will produce both black and chocolate, in a constant ratio. Twenty-five percent of their litters will inherit black from both parents, so they will be black and be true-breeding for this color. Another 25% will inherit chocolate from both parents and will be true-breeding chocolates. The remaining 50% will be apparent blacks still carrying the recessive chocolate color and will produce black and chocolate young in the ratio previously mentioned.

For the sake of clarity, colors and patterns of color can be divided into groups. These are: Agouti, Black, Chocolate, and Yellow. Additional mutations influence these colors and produce specific markings and patterns. These are known as the Marked varieties, and the Fox and Tan mice.

THE AGOUTI GROUP

In this group are the Golden Agouti, the Cinnamon, and the Chinchilla. They possess a pattern of color. The Golden Agouti is a cultivated color of the wild mouse. The Cinnamon mouse has the black pigment absent from the Agouti pattern. This gives the appearance of a Chocolate mouse with yellow-tipped hairs, called ticking. The Chinchilla factor causes an extreme dilution of the yellow in the Agouti pattern, giving the characteristic white-tipped hairs in the Chinchilla mouse. Each of these colors resulted from a mutation, or change, of the Agouti pattern factor.

THE BLACK GROUP

The mice in this group are called Selfs, meaning of one color. They have no color pattern, resulting in the blending of the three basic colors. Black being the densest concentration of color, the mice are solid black. A mutation called blue dilution dilutes the black color to a bluish gray as seen in the Blue mouse. Pink-eyed dilution, another mutation, when present in both parents, further dilutes the black color, resulting in the Dove mouse. It will have ruby eyes.

A good specimen of a mouse is sound in size, type, and stamina.

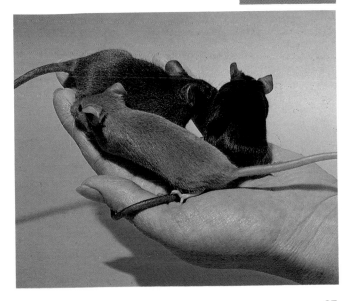

27

THE CHOCOLATE GROUP

These are self-colored mice, and the color is also affected by the action of blue dilution and pink-eyed dilution. The Self-Chocolate mouse has no black pigment in its makeup, so it has a rich chocolate color with very deep ruby eyes best seen against a strong light background. Blue dilution changes the chocolate color to a bluish brown. The pink eyes of the Champagne mouse show the presence of pink-eyed dilution, and as the name suggests, the coat is the color of champagne.

THE YELLOW GROUP

Red, Fawn, and Cream are the colors in this group. Reds of exhibition quality should be the color of an Irish Setter dog. The Fawn mouse with a gold yellow coat with pink eyes is a Red mouse diluted by the pink-eyed dilution factor. Blue dilution, acting on the red color, creates the delicate shade of the Cream mouse, which has black eyes.

THE MARKED VARIETIES

In this group are mice with spots of one color or another set on a contrasting background of white. They can be bred in any of the self colors. The markings tend to gravitate toward complete coloration or a minimum of coloring, and a balance is difficult to maintain. Mice of this variety are seen with the familiar Dutch-marked pattern or in an even-marked or broken-marked pattern. Other marked mice are the Variegated mouse and the Black-eyed White, which is a marked mouse with all the color selectively bred out of its coat. The only pigment visible is seen in the eyes, which are black.

TANS

A striking contrast between a rich tan belly color topped by any of the accepted self colors makes the Tan mouse a most popular variety. These are Tan mice affected by a mutation that preserves the tan belly color of the Agouti pattern.

FOXES

These are actually Tan mice with the addition of the Chinchilla mutation. As the Chinchilla factor bleaches

yellow to a near white, a white belly with ticked flanks makes its appearance. These, too, are bred in most of the self colors. (Both the Tan and Fox mice have a sharp line of demarcation

A fourteen-day-old youngster.

where the two colors meet.)

THE ALBINO OR PINK-EYED WHITE MOUSE

The traits of the Albino mouse have long been a source of confusion to the fancier. This mouse differs from the self mouse in that it cannot express the recessive color it has inherited. This ability has been lost through the effects of a mutation that prevents the mouse from showing the color it really possesses. However, since it does have a color background, when it is mated to a colored mouse the color becomes evident. As there is almost an infinite number of colors in the fancy today, you can see that there are just as many different kinds of Albino mice. As this trait is recessive, both parents must carry it in order to litter a nest of Albino youngsters.

OTHER ODD MUTATIONS

Yellow mice store their pigment in fatty tissues in the body, pigments known as lipochromes. These mice can become obese or very fat and are hard to keep in a trim condition. This tendency can be regulated to an extent by a rigid diet and selective breeding. Creams having less intensive pigmentation are less affected in this respect.

The possible color and coat mutations of the mouse are limitless.

Varieties

Regardless of the color of the mouse, it must have certain physical characters to be a good representative of its breed.

The mouse should be seven to eight inches from the tip possible between them showing a good width of skull. The body should be long and narrow, slightly arched over the loins and should give an appearance of raciness and alert attention.

of the nose to the end of the tail, and the tail should be about as long as the body. The mouse must have a long body with a long clean head, not too fine or pointed at the nose. The eyes should be large and prominent, the ears large and tulip shaped, carried erect and forward with as much space as

The tail must be free from kinks and should be well set on at the root, gradually tapering like a whip lash to a fine end. The coat should be short, smooth, and glossy and show no tendency to bristle. The mouse should show no evidence of physical defects or unsteady temperament.

Chinchilla mouse. In general, the more your mouse is handled, the more he will become accustomed to your touch.

31

The mouse fancy recognizes over 30 standarized colors and varieties of colored mice. While many other colors and combinations of color occasionally appear, these other colors have not been standardized as not enough interest has been shown to warrant their being recognized by the fancy. The standardized varieties of mice can be divided as follows: the self or whole-colored mice, the marked varieties, Tans, Foxes, and the A.O.V. or Any Other Variety.

SELF BLACK

These mice have the most dense pigmentation of all the varieties of fancy mice. The color is velvety black, deep and lustrous. All areas of the body not covered by hair contain the black pigment, including the nose, feet, ears, and tail. White toenails and tail tips are considered to be a fault. The coat must be completely free of white or tan hairs. These are frequent around the vent and not difficult to observe. However, cross-bred matings will often introduce tan hairs and objectionable rusty flanks.

SELF BLUE

Black mice, having blue dilution in duplex, will appear as Self Blues. Simply speaking, these are Self Blacks with less dense pigmentation. While black can only be black, when it is diluted it can be seen in various shades and intensities of color. The ideal calls for a medium shade of slate blue covering all parts of the body. If they are too light they will have a silvery cast to their coat, the first sign of poor quality in Blues. For this reason keep a few darker colored mice for breeders. This will enable you to keep the color in balance, as you mate the darker Blues to the lighter mice to give a medium shade of blue so admired.

SELF DOVE

Pink-eyed dilution acting on the self black colors

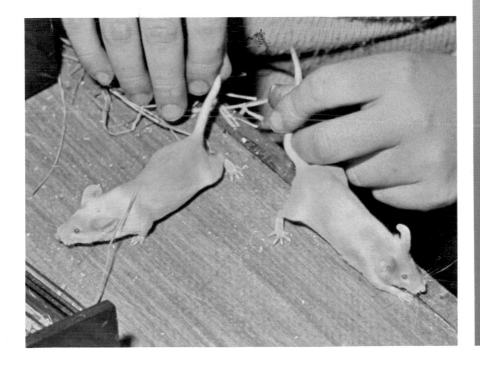

A pair of Self Dove mice.

33

further dilutes the color, resulting in the Dove mouse. The desired color is a soft dove gray. Again, this color must be kept in balance using both the lighter and darker colors. Strive to keep the belly color as deep as the top coat. In the past, some organizations gave a separate classification to the Lilac mouse, but as it resembles the Dove mouse, they decided to eliminate it as a separate mouse color category. Both have ruby eyes, although the Lilac is a Chocolate mouse with pink-eyed dilution.

SELF CHOCOLATE

This is a color recommended for the novice as it consistently breeds true to form. The mouse should be near the color of unsweetened baking chocolate, with the color extending down into the skin. While the eyes appear to be black, a strong light will prove them to be a deep ruby color. This color lasts well with age, and if your breeders are from pure stock, they will reward you with litters of the same excellent color.

SELF CHAMPAGNE

Always a favorite, the Champagne mouse with its pink eyes and sleek fur the color of sparkling champagne ranks near the top of preference by fanciers. Consistent good color and excellent type seem to characterize the Champagne mouse. The clean warm color is enhanced by a pink cast running throughout the coat. Avoid breeding those with a light muzzle or belly as they will eventually produce young with an objectionable mealy or mottled color. Because of the pink-eyed dilution factor, the mouse can properly be called a Pink-eyed Chocolate.

SELF RED

Here is an outstanding example of the breeder's art. The typical Red mouse is the color of an Irish Setter dog, although many variations of the color are commonly seen. A Red mouse is difficult to produce in a combination of sound color and good type. They tend to be too compact, with short tails and ears, and the ideal streamlined type is noticeably absent in Red mice. The main reason for this fault is because they have a strong tendency to be overweight, and adult specimens are seldom seen in a trim condition. This can be avoided, in part, by careful attention to their diet and selective breeding when pairing up the parent stock. Agouti and Chocolate young occasionally crop up in their litters.

SELF FAWN

Red parents both having pink-eyed dilution in their

Mice are merry little creatures that can be most entertaining.

background will produce Pink-eyed Reds or Fawns in their litters. They have a rich golden color somewhat like a carrot. They possess good type comparable to other varieties, and the color is outstanding in the finished coat. A point to watch for in the breeding pens is a pale belly color. Such mice should not be considered for future breeding stock.

This Black and White Pied mouse projects overall good health: a shining coat, bright eyes, and an alert appearance.

A Long-haired
Pied mouse.

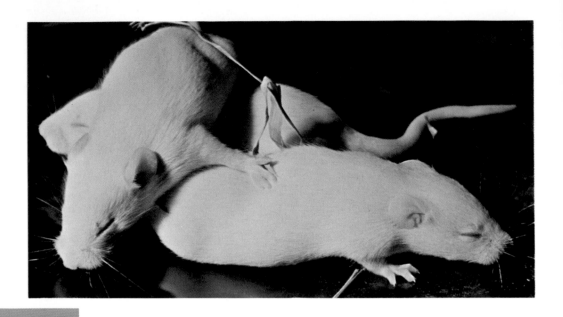

SELF CREAM

Further dilution of the red color, aided by the blue dilution factor, brings to the fancier the Cream mouse. The black eyes of this mouse contrast with the delicate color of the rich cream coat, creating a most pleasing combination. Some creams are too dark, approaching the color of the Dove mouse, and it is the lightest shades that should be the goal. Creams have been developed to a very high degree, and their size and shape are close to the ideal. This is a variety for the specialist.

Some organizations, such as the American Fancy Rat and Mouse Association, also recognize the following self colors: beige, gold, lilac, orange, silver, and white.

PINK-EYED WHITE (OR ALBINO)

The Pink-eyed White has been in the hands of fanciers for many years, and the type and style of this mouse have been so well established that it is widely used as an outcross to other varieties to improve conformation. A good White cannot be improved upon for color purity, so the care exercised in providing clean breeding pens is often the narrow margin between fine mice and excellent mice. Pen stains show up readily, so their cages must be kept immaculate to preserve the snowy white coat color. It is safe to say that more Pink-eyed White mice have been bred than any other variety.

DUTCH-MARKED

This is the familiar color pattern seen in the Dutch-marked rabbit. The forward half of the body will be white, with the exception of the cheek patches. These are located on both sides of the head and include the ears, upper jowls, and the area immediately forward of the eyes. The cheek patches should be separated by a narrow blaze of white between the ears and a white area underneath the jaws. The saddle on the rear half of the body should be a solid color and should extend well into the tail and down into the rear legs. The remaining area of the feet and tail should be white. The lines of demarcation where the color ends in the feet and tail are known as the stops. While most Dutch mice present a good appearance on the top side, it is the underside of the saddle that is often ragged and tends to lag toward the rear in an uneven line. This ragged line is

Mice reach maturity at approximately 12 weeks of age.

called a slip. Dutch mice can be bred in any of the self colors, but the black and chocolate colors are most widely bred. They are usually of the same outstanding type as the self or A.O.V. mice. The young mice are selected at a very early age for the desired good markings, but type cannot be selected at this age. This same comment applies to all the marked varieties.

BROKEN-MARKED

The Broken-marked mouse has an irregular pattern of spots on the body and must have a single spot or nose patch on either side of the head. The spots should be even in size and must be well dispersed over the entire body. The number and placings of the spots determine the worth of the mouse, but a good six-spot mouse is considered better than a ten-spot mouse with brindled or streaked patches of color.

EVEN-MARKED

This mouse differs from the Broken-marked mouse in

the placement of the spots, which must be set in a balanced pattern on both sides of the body. Almost all Even-marked mice originate from litters of Broken-marked mice, but it should be possible to create a strain with the tendency toward the even distribution of spots. They are seldom seen.

VARIEGATED

The body color of this mouse is white covered with small splashes of pigment. The drawback to this variety is that the pigmented areas tend to form in clumps, especially around the sides of the head and the rump. Proper selection of breeding stock will help in this respect, but this is a variety for the specialist who is willing to devote much time toward the perfection of the proper pattern of color.

BLACK-EYED WHITE

The Black-eyed White is actually a marked mouse with the color selectively bred out of it except for the black pigment seen in the eyes. As the elimination of body color was accomplished by intensive inbreeding, the mouse lacks the ideal size and type. This makes them

A particularly attractive variety of mouse is the Siamese mouse. Ideally, the Siamese mouse should exhibit a harmonious balance between body color, shadings, and points.

A Sliver mouse. Note the delicate quality of this animal's coloration.

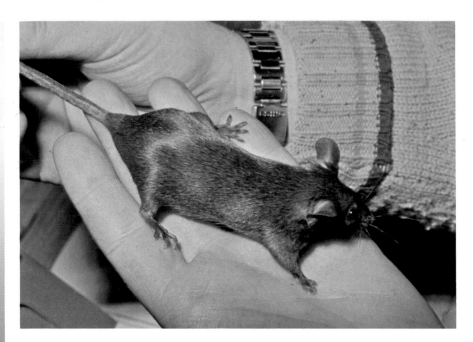

A Golden Agouti mouse. The golden effect in the coat of this variety is created by yellow pigmentation in the hairs.

inferior in these respects to the Pink-eyed Whites, which excel in this respect. An allowance should be made for the fact that they are really one of the marked varieties. A percentage of their litters will have markings similar to Variegated mice.

TANS

The striking contrast of a rich tan belly color topped by a sparkling self color makes the Tan mouse a most popular variety. The tan color should be barely visible when viewed from the side, and it should run in a straight line along the flanks of the animal and should include the chest and underside of the jaw. The tan should cease abruptly where it meets the top color and should not taper off in a brindling effect. When the mouse stands erect it exhibits its remarkable color pattern at its best. They are bred in any of the recognized self colors, and the Golden Agouti with a tan belly is listed as an Agouti-tan. The blacks are the most popular, followed closely by the chocolates and the dilutes of these two self colors. Any of the self varieties can be tanned by a simple cross with a Tan mouse of the same color, but any selfs obtained from these matings should not be used for breeding, for they will introduce scattered tan hairs in their litters.

FOXES

Fox mice are similar to the Tan mice in their color pattern. However, the belly color is white instead of tan, and there must be a slight ticking on the flanks of the mouse. They can be had in most of the self colors. They were originally produced by a cross of Tan and Chinchilla mice. (The chinchilla factor bleaches the yellow or tan undercolor to a near white.)

A.O.V. GROUP

These mice have distinctive color patterns and markings, and they exhibit an array of color combinations seen in no other group. Some of these patterns are evident only under close observation as the difference in the colors is subtle, while others are startling and outstanding in their contrast. The following varieties are included in the A.O.V. group.

A Seal Point Siamese mouse.

A Blue Tan mouse. Good Tans exhibit a belly color that is of a rich golden hue.

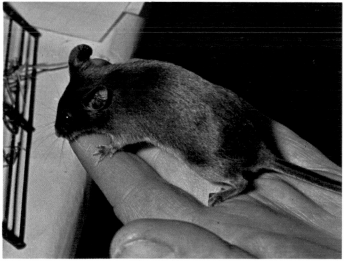

A Chocolate
White Rump
mouse.

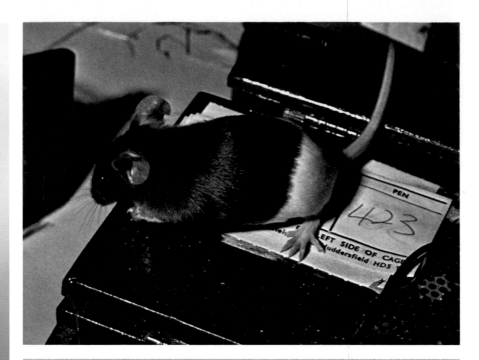

A Long-haired
Pied Cream
mouse.

A black Tan mouse. This variety of mouse is named for the prominent tan coloration of its underside.

The different possibilities in patterns and markings are one of the exciting aspects of mouse breeding.

A very attractive color variety is that of the Sable mouse.

Fawn Satin mouse. The care and attention that you give to your pet will be reflected in the animal's general condition.

Opposite: A Cream mouse.

Sable This is another variety with a color pattern similar to that of the Tan mouse. They must have a top color of a deep, rich, dark brown appearing as a near black. This dark area covering the back and the top of the head is sometimes called the saddle. This dark saddle gradually blends into the tan of the belly, and there is no sharp line of demarcation where the colors meet as seen in the Tans and Foxes. The flanks are covered with a mixture of tan and dark brown hairs.

Chinchilla This mouse first appeared in some experimental laboratory

mouse stock, and the appearance of this color mutation was a lucky one for the fancier. This color pattern allowed other varieties to be introduced to the mouse fancy. The familiar Chinchilla rabbit is a good example of the coloring demanded by the standard. The silvery undercoat tipped by dark brown or black gives a soft finished look to the mouse. The belly color is white, and this three-color combination is in a class by itself.

Cinnamon Cinnamon mice have another unusual color pattern. The undercoat is chocolate, topped by yellow-tipped hairs called ticking.

NEW TYPES OF MICE

Today's mouse fanciers are enjoying success and recognition in the development of new types of mice. Two newcomers that are generating excitement in the fancy are the Blue Point Siamese mouse and the Brindled mouse.

A Champagne mouse. This variety of mouse is one of the most popular of mouse varieties.

Rex mouse.

Training

Opposite:
Patience and
consistency are
important
elements in
training.

The mouse is an
energetic and
nimble little
fellow who loves
to explore his
surroundings.

If mice are handled frequently, they soon lose any trace of fear and can be taught to perform a number of tricks with a minimum of effort. When you are teaching a mouse a new trick or to perform a simple task, keep in mind that your little pet is not able to reason and that it relies upon instinct to tell it how to react.

A mouse is very sure-footed and will climb a toy ladder readily if it starts its journey from the center of the ladder. The mouse will immediately climb to the top and then down without a misstep. If a favorite bit of food is placed at the top, it will learn to scamper up the ladder as soon as it comes near the toy. Another easy trick for your mouse to attempt is tightrope walking. Here is where your pet will excel, for it has a marvelous sense of balance and will use its tail to maintain its balance

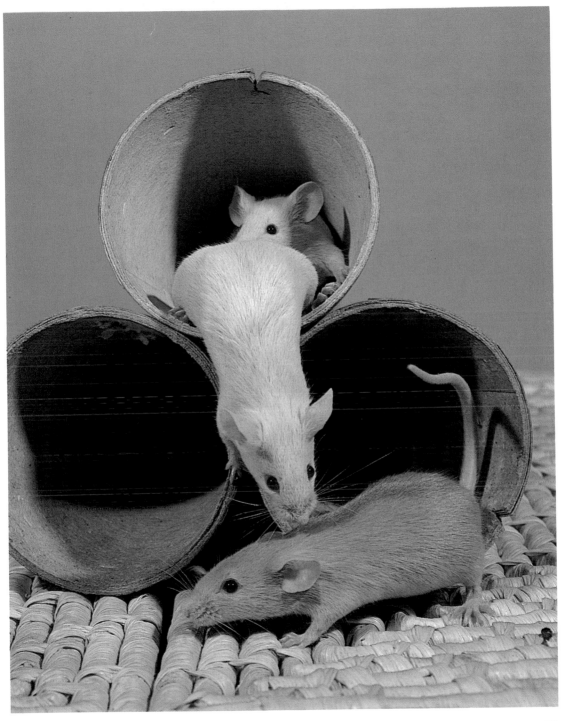

much as a circus performer would use a parasol. The mouse may pause on the trip over the length of rope, grip the rope with its hind feet, and stand erect and look around with little or no concern. Of course, you will want to keep the rope but a few inches from a surface so that if the mouse should slip and fall it will not hurt itself.

A variation of tightrope walking can be had by teaching your litle performer to climb a rope held in a vertical position. The mouse may decide to reverse its direction after climbing up for a while. Watch how it will carefully change the position of its feet and, with the tail wrapped securely around the rope, cautiously inch its way down to a solid surface. If each mouse is allowed to exercise and perform on a table top in the

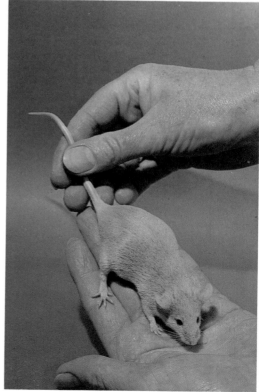

Your pet shop stocks a variety of play items specially designed to occupy and amuse your pet.

house, they will have a more secure feeling and be unafraid. Mice become uneasy when exposed to direct sunlight, as their instinct tells them that they can be seen by natural enemies; they will try to find a hiding place and will not concentrate on the more important things that you are attempting to teach them.

Several mice can be grouped together for a race toward a distant goal. The length of the race will be determined by the size of the table top. Narrow strips of

Mice are among the easiest pets to care for.

cardboard or wood should be used to separate the mice entered in the race as they travel from one end of the course to the other. One mouse may go in a straight line and be far ahead of the others and then decide to double back to the starting line, or it may climb over the fence and visit its neighbor; so the outcome of each race is always in doubt. A secret way to train a mouse for races is to reward it with food placed at the goal. Once the mouse learns this point, it will always beat the rest of the contestants to the finish line, unless your opponent has also trained his track

Because of their entertaining mannerisms, mice are interesting to observe.

Never force your little pet to do more than he is capable of doing.

Tame mice can maneuver themselves about in a surprisingly skillful fashion.

Mice are notorious nibblers who will "sample" just about anything!

A mouse should not be picked up in this manner.

Opposite: The time you spend caring for your pet will be more than compensated for by the enjoyment he gives you.

The mouse uses its tail to maintain its sense of balance.

stars in the same manner.

An equally amusing trick for mice to learn is to be able to travel through a maze of obstructions toward a goal. This will take longer for the mouse to learn, as it must remember which path leads to a blind end. If a food treat is the reward for a successful journey through the maze, the mouse will eventually learn to travel the course quite rapidly.

Handle your mice with kindness and patience and never try to force them to do more than their small minds can grasp. Guard against accidental falls and never allow them to run on the

floor as they are apt to be injured if they squeeze into small openings or under low furniture. I have mentioned some of the ways in which mice can be trained, but I am sure that you will think of many more things to teach your pets to do and they will entertain and amuse you for hours in the process.

I should not close this chapter without mentioning "waltzing" mice. A waltzing mouse has a very poor sense of balance or equilibrium so that it cannot walk or run in a straight line. In trying to gain its balance, a waltzer will sway to one side, then to the other and suddenly whirl around in a dizzy circle for a few revolutions and just as suddenly resume an erratic forward direction. This makes them interesting in an odd way, and they don't require training to do their "trick."

Mousekeeping is a hobby that can be an enriching and educational experience.

Index